Patterson Elementary School
3731 Lawrence Drive
Naperville, IL 60564

108386 EN
Milk, Yogurt, and Cheese

Green, Emily K.
ATOS BL 1.9
Points: 0.5

LG

THE NEW FOOD GUIDE PYRAMID

Milk,
Yogurt, and Cheese

by Emily K. Green

BLASTOFF!
READERS
2

BELLWETHER MEDIA • MINNEAPOLIS, MN

Note to Librarians, Teachers, and Parents:

Blastoff! Readers are carefully developed by literacy experts and combine standards-based content with developmentally appropriate text.

Level 1 provides the most support through repetition of high-frequency words, light text, predictable sentence patterns, and strong visual support.

Level 2 offers early readers a bit more challenge through varied simple sentences, increased text load, and less repetition of high-frequency words.

Level 3 advances early-fluent readers toward fluency through increased text and concept load, less reliance on visuals, longer sentences, and more literary language.

Whichever book is right for your reader, Blastoff! Readers are the perfect books to build confidence and encourage a love of reading that will last a lifetime!

This edition first published in 2007 by Bellwether Media.

Library of Congress Cataloging-in-Publication Data
Green, Emily K., 1966–
  Milk, yogurt, and cheese / by Emily K. Green.
    p. cm. – (Blastoff! readers) (New food guide pyramid)
  ISBN-10: 1-60014-000-9 (hardcover : alk. paper)
  ISBN-13: 978-1-60014-000-6 (hardcover : alk. paper)
  1. Dairy products in human nutrition–Juvenile literature. 2. Nutrition–Juvenile literature. I. Title. II. Series.
  QP144.M54G74 2007
  613.2–dc22   2006000567

Text copyright © 2007 by Bellwether Media.
Printed in the United States of America.

Table of Contents

The **food guide pyramid** can help you choose healthy foods.

The Food Guide Pyramid

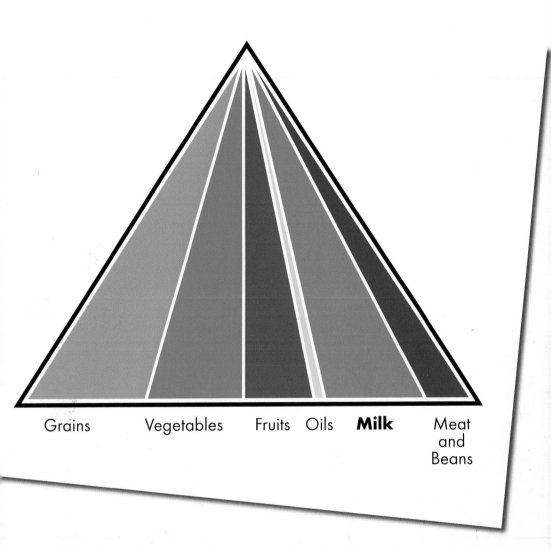

Grains   Vegetables   Fruits   Oils   **Milk**   Meat and Beans

Each color stripe stands for a food group. The blue stripe is for the milk group.

The milk group includes milk, yogurt, and cheese.

Milk comes from cows
or goats.

Yogurt is made from milk.

Cheese is made from milk.

Milk, yogurt, and cheese have **protein**.

Protein helps you build strong **muscles**.

Milk, yogurt, and cheese have **calcium**.

Calcium makes your bones
strong so you can play
and grow.

3

Kids should have three cups
from the milk group
every day.

14

So ask for milk at your next meal. You will be glad you did.

Pour milk on your cereal for breakfast.

Eat cheese or yogurt for a snack.

Remember to choose milk, yogurt, or cheese that is low in **fat**.

18

You will feel great when you choose low-fat foods from the milk group every day.

19

How Much Should A Kid Eat Each Day?

Vegetables
2 ½ cups

Milk, Yogurt, & Cheese
3 cups

Grains
6 servings

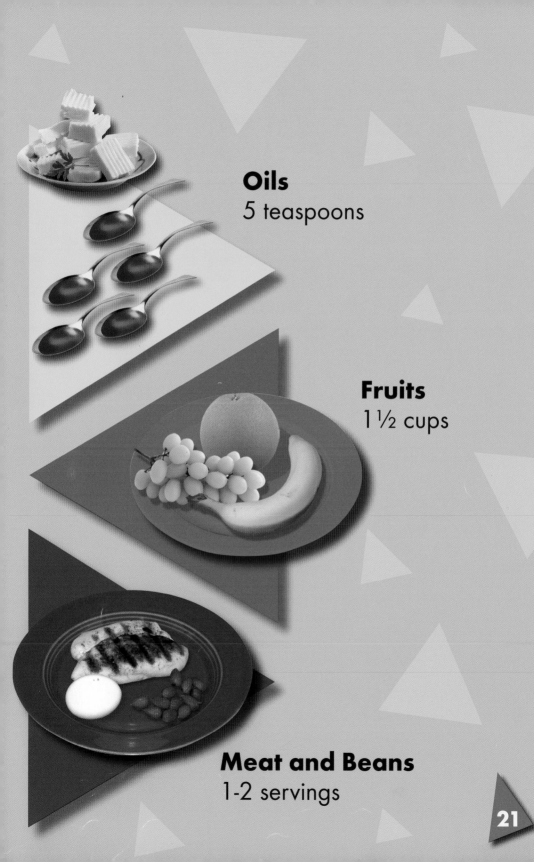

Oils
5 teaspoons

Fruits
1 ½ cups

Meat and Beans
1-2 servings

Glossary

calcium—a part of some foods that your body needs for building strong bones and teeth

fat—a part of some foods that gives you energy and helps your body use vitamins

food guide pyramid—a chart showing the kinds and amounts of foods you should eat each day

muscles—the parts of your body that help you move

protein—the building blocks of your bones, muscles, skin and blood

To Learn More

AT THE LIBRARY

Aliki. *Milk: From Cow to Carton.* New York: HarperTrophy, 1992.

Zemlicka, Shannon. *From Milk to Cheese.* Minneapolis, Minn.: Lerner, 2003.

Rockwell, Lizzy. *Good Enough to Eat: A Kid's Guide to Food And Nutrition.* New York: HarperCollins, 1999.

ON THE WEB

Learning more about healthy eating is as easy as 1, 2, 3.

1. Go to www.factsurfer.com

2. Enter "healthy eating" into search box.

3. Click the "Surf" button and you will see a list of related web sites.

With factsurfer.com, finding more information is just a click away.

Index

The photographs in this book are reproduced through the courtesy of: Jack Andersen/Food Pix, front cover; Ken Chernus/Getty Images, p. 4; Michael Rosenfeld/Getty Images, p. 6; Joe Gough, p. 7; Paul Webster/Getty Images, p. 8; Maryse Raymond/Getty Images, p. 9; Olga Lyubkina, p. 10; Gudelia Marmion, p. 11; Butch Martin/Getty Images, pp. 12-13; Pat LaCroix/Getty Images, p. 14; Anne Ackermann/Getty Images, p. 15; Alan Egginton, p. 16; Juan Silva/Getty Images, p. 17; altrendo images/Getty Images, p. 18; White Cross Productions/Getty Images, p. 19; Juan Martinez, p. 20(top); Olga Lyubkina, p. 20(middle); Tim McClellan, p.20(bottom), p. 21(middle, bottom); Michael Rosenfeld/Getty Images, p.21(top).

Patterson Elementary School
3731 Lawrence Drive
Naperville, IL 60564